OVERCOMING
SATANIC
ENTANGLEMENTS

Apostle Stephen A. Garner

Overcoming Satanic Entanglements

Unless otherwise indicated, all scriptural quotations are taken from the *King James Version* of the Holy Bible. All Hebraic and Greek definitions are taken from the *Strong's Exhaustive Concordance*.

ISBN # 978-1981788637
Printed in the United States of America

Table of Contents

Preface

One of the most potent aspects of prayer that I believe will cause us to excel in our assignment is sight. Intercessors and those burdened with the mandate of eternity to pray have intentionally developed their sight.

The utterances heaven wants to loose in the earth most often are connected to how we see. In Jeremiah 1:1 the Lord asked Jeremiah, what do you see? Jeremiah's sight was activated and he was able to declare what was revealed to him.

The dealings of God are increasing amidst those called to eternal partnership with Christ in prayer. Heaven is carving out sensitivity and grace is surging for intercession.

The root systems that are entangling multitudes globally are coming under severe scrutiny and destruction. God is overwhelming these systems with His power because of the unceasing prayers of the saints.

Poise yourselves and get ready for a great outpouring because heaven has been provoked to move in the earth because of the prayers of the righteous.

INTRODUCTION

This book came as a result of an early morning whisper from the LORD. Over the years of growing in prayer, I normally receive prayer burdens from words that the LORD speaks to my spirit. The last several years' many things have been birthed, wisdom imparted, insight gained or new assignments revealed from early morning encounters.

On December 4th, 2017 around 3:30 a.m. I heard the word entangled so loud and clear. After wrestling with sleeplessness for another hour or so the word entangled came again. This time I was moved to meditate on it and mark it as a word of urgency.

Later that morning, I was conversing with one of my leaders and the word entangled emerged in our conversation. It was in the context of iniquitywhich means twistedthing or perversity. My spirit was stirred as I sensed the LORD wanting to activate a measure of breakthrough for our local church.

As we conversed further I received greater insight and began praying for certain spiritual sons of mine. There was a tremendous release of grace for intercession that came upon me and I began to ask the LORD to judge the demonic entanglements, which I perceived had overwhelmed them for years. Afterwards I knew an obstruction was removed and liberty was prevailing.

I'm now stirred to put prayers together to encourage you to intercede for deliverance from webs, nets and twisted things bent on limiting your progression through demonic entanglements.

The word for entangle in the Greek, key G1758, is enecho means to hold in or upon, i.e. ensnare; by implication, to keep a grudge: entangle with, have a quarrel against, urge.

There are countless people in the Body of Christ held in captivity even though Christ has set them free. They have experienced holds and restraints placed upon them in certain areas of their walk.

Others have succumbed to snares and traps set for them by the powers of darkness.

There are some who also find themselves governed by grudges or quarrels intrinsically with their inadequacies or externally with other people. These grudges and quarrels often times promote urges that further entangle the believer.

These entanglements eventually morph into satanic yokes that have been placed upon many of us unbeknownst to us. These yokes serve as the product of Satanic entanglements.

Some yokes come as a result of bloodline issues; some are societal issues, relational and spiritual issues.

May the prayers from this book provoke heaven to respond and provoke hell to loose you in Jesus Name.

CHAPTER 1

OVERCOMING ENTANGLEMENTS OF BONDAGE

Galatians 5:1 KJV
Stand fast therefore in the liberty
wherewith Christ hath made us free, and be
not ENTANGLED AGAIN WITH
THE YOKE OF BONDAGE.

The Spirit of the LORD is a proponent of liberty. His presence within the life of a believer is to liberate them from all works active to bind and restrict them from obeying and serving God.

Satan however, prior to salvation set up an elaborate system of entanglements and network of demonic roots to keep the soul and future of the believer in captivity.

Understanding that liberty is of God and that He wants us free in every area of our lives is imperative to our walk in Christ and destiny. May His liberating power surge in your life as you begin praying these prayers.

LORD empower me to stand fast in the liberty of Christ.

LORD cause my feet to be firmly positioned in You.

It is written whosoever the son sets free, is free in deed.

I decree freedom obtained through the shed blood of Christ.

I decree the blood of Christ purges my mind and conscience from every dead work active to restrain my purpose.

LORD, anoint my eyes with salve and cause me to see every plan deployed to place demonic holds on my life.

I renounce all temptations and urges of darkness sent to put yokes of iron on me.

LORD, send your fire and deliver me from every scheme of hell working to secure my captivity.

I will not be entangled with any yoke that propagates bondage or captivity.

I decree every Satanic root system established in my soul comes under divine scrutiny and fierce judgment in Jesus Name.

Every demonic entanglement working to interfere with my liberty in Christ succumbs to fires of judgment in Jesus Name.

All discord and contention in my soul working to ensnare me by bents and vices are neutralized by fire.

I receive an impartation of strength to stand in the liberty of Christ. I decree freedom is my portion.

I renounce all ambition that would foster my demise or trap my life.

I decree every strategy and hidden agenda working to ensnare my soul is burned by fire.

I command all yokes from my background and family line are neutralized by the blood of Jesus Christ.

Every cord placed upon my emotions, serving as a source of entanglement, is severed from my life in Jesus Name.

CHAPTER 2

OVERCOMING THE AFFAIRS OF THIS LIFE

2 Timothy 2:3-4 KJV
Thou therefore endure hardness, as a good soldier of Jesus Christ. 4 No man that warreth ENTANGLETH HIMSELF WITH THE AFFAIRS OF THIS LIFE; that he may please him who hath chosen him to be a soldier.

Hardness, afflictions and suffering come with living a godly life. Many believers who encounter seasons and times of suffering can easily be shipwreck because they don't equate living godly and suffering as a

11

packaged deal. 1 Peter 4 emphasizes this truth.

Suffering for righteousness sake helps develop the soul of the believer to live godly at all times. Satan will seek to exploit the believer during these times and pervert our destiny. His aim is to use the world, as it relates to material things, in order to entangle us and thus provoke us to turn away from God.

I agree with you for an abundance of grace to properly disengage from the material kingdom. I decree that as you pray these prayers God will judge all entanglements rooted in the world and affairs connected to your natural life in Jesus Name.

I receive grace to endure hard times, suffering and afflictions in Jesus Name.

I renounce any and all weariness, battle fatigue, fainting and destiny aborting strategies of hell in Jesus Name.

I claim wisdom to endure and forbid any surges of darkness in my life.

LORD release strength upon me to endure and prevail in Jesus Name.

LORD send a fresh wind upon me as a renewed zeal to function as a good soldier in Jesus Name.

Every unauthorized allegiance and connection to this life and its tenants are broken in Jesus Name.

LORD I proclaim fidelity to You alone.

I renounce any infidelity working in my appetites and desires to ensnare me with the world in Jesus Name.

Father bring every lust and evil appetite, active in my members, under judgment by fire.

All affairs of this life seeking to subvert and entangle me are burned by fire in Jesus Name.

Every yoke working with cares and concerns beyond my measure urging me to react be broken in Jesus Name.

Every setup and prevailing false burdens are broken off of my life.

I renounce all lust inspired appetites and contemptible behavior, working to pervertmy soul through the affairs of this life, in Jesus Name.

LORD I claim refuge in you and decree the ensuing chaos of this life is forbidden access.

I'm crucified with Christ and decree the life I now live brings pleasure to you LORD.

CHAPTER 3

OVERCOMING THE ENTANGLEMENTS OF THE LAND

Exodus 14:3 KJV
For Pharaoh will say of the children of Israel, They are ENTANGLED IN THE LAND, the wilderness hath shut them in.

Pharaoh was a type of strongman that ruled over Israel while they were in Egyptian captivity. Israel spent 430 years in Egypt and they served under the harsh cruelty of taskmasters. God began to move by His sovereignty and with systematic plagues,He superimposed His power upon the demonic agenda, against His people, in the land of Egypt.

Notice how Pharaoh declares that Israel is entangled in the land and the wilderness hath shut them in. There are demonic forces active in every plot of geography on this planet and none are exempt. For instance, if there is violence that has plagued a territorial grid for any period of time eventually the lives of the citizens of the land in general will be affected. Innocent families will get entangled in the vicious web of violence and thus further perpetuate the pain and agony associated with violence.

God wants to burn and consume all entanglements imposed upon us and our families as it relates to the land we are joined to. He wants to open every pathway associated with the powers of the land seeking to ensnare us and hold us captive. I

decree that the territorial powers of your grid that are active to entangle and shut you in, are overthrown and decimated by the power of God in Jesus Name.

By the Spirit of Christ who dwells within me I renounce the rule and voice of Pharaoh seeking to ensnare me in my land.

Every taskmaster deployed against my lineage and bloodline is displaced by the fire of God, I decree we excel and prosper in our territorial grids in Jesus Name.

All edicts of Pharaoh and his magicians against my liberty in Christ are overturned.

I decree every voice of opposition against my advancement is cut off in Jesus Name.

All oppressive words working to subdue me in my territory and the lands I'm sent to fail miserably in Jesus Name.

I will not be entangled in my place of inheritance and acquisition of land ordained for me by God.

I decree the land upon which I dwell will yield its increase.

I decree all crooked and perverse agendas programmed in the land, on which I stand, are broken asunder in Jesus Name.

I will not be restricted in my city or the regions I'm sent to.

I decree the resources of the land come to me freely and without fail because my God has gone before me and burns up all resistance in Jesus Name.

All entrapments active to shut me up and restrict my growth and productivity is now destroyed in Jesus Name.

Every work of injustice and entanglement of bondage in my sphere of influence is crushed today by the power of God.

I decree all evil covenants forged in blood, on the land I dwell in assigned against my destiny are overturned and dissolved in the Name of Jesus.

Father liberate me from all evil vices perpetuated by my family on the land which I stand. Let not their transgression interfere with Your plans for my life in Jesus Name.

I command all spirits of the land working to prohibit my elevation and breakthrough to be bound in Jesus Name.

CHAPTER 4

OVERCOMING ENTANGLEMENTS AGAINST MY WORDS

Matthew 22:15 KJV
Then went the Pharisees, and took counsel
how they might ENTANGLE HIM
IN HIS TALK.

Jesus declares that His words are spirit and life. His utterance and decrees influence both the natural and spirit realms. There are dark powers bent on entangling us with our words. The LORD tell His disciples in John 14:30 that He wouldn't speak with them because the prince of this world was coming, but nothing to the contrary would be found in Him.

I believe that part of Christ descending into the lower parts of the earth wasto reclaim the keys of death and hell. He accomplished that and has risen with all power. I believe Jesus has successfully neutralized every indictment and accusation that Satan could use against us in part because His speech was above reproach.

Even though Christ has overcome the evil one and confirmed our salvation, hell is still bent on entangling us in our speech. 2 Corinthians 4:13 emphasizes the fact that we are to speak as we believe. Ensnarements and entanglements, often work when believers talk and dialogue contrary to our faith. I'm agreeing with heaven for the sustainability of your words and decreeing that the tongue of the learned would be your portion in Jesus Name.

Father, expose and bring to naught the collusions of every Pharisee spirit deployed against me to entangle me with my words.

I decree every gathering and counsel of the wicked, collaborating and working to entangle me, is judged by the hand of God.

All mockery and evil surmising enacted against me is cutoff in Jesus Name.

Accusations against my soul fall to the ground and die in Jesus Name.

All psychic prayers and words loosed to manipulate my soul are cast down in Jesus Name.

Every secret counsel of the workers of insurrection and adjutants of hell are exposed in Jesus Name.

I decree I will not be entangled in my speech but my words will be forceful and precise.

I decree the voice of the LORD flows through me with great clarity.

I proclaim grace resting on me for proper and accurate articulation of the things of God.

I decree words of wisdom and knowledge are manifesting through me without fail as I open my mouth to proclaim the purposes of God.

Every weapon formed against my voice to ensnare and suppress it is rendered inoperative in Jesus Name.

All pressure tactics of hell loosed to twist my words and create havoc, because of verbal indiscretions, are rooted out of my life by fire in Jesus Name.

CAMBRIDGE BIBLES

Four Centuries of Craftsmanship

Cambridge University Press is the oldest publisher in the world. The Press's first Bible, printed in 1591, was an edition of the Geneva Bible – the translation that crossed to America with the Pilgrim Fathers. Thus was established the renowned Cambridge tradition of Bible publishing, still unbroken after more than four hundred years.

Cambridge University Press remains committed to the highest standards of printing and binding. The finest Cambridge Bibles may be bound in one of a variety of styles of real leather, the material traditionally chosen for the most highly esteemed books. Not only does leather have an intrinsic aesthetic appeal, but it also offers the best protection for important texts.

Please retain this information slip and your receipt or other proof of purchase, for the benefit of the vendor or Cambridge University Press, in the unlikely event that you later have need to contact either about this Bible within the period covered by the limited warranty.

Limited Warranty

The full text of the limited warranty on Cambridge Bibles is available at **www.cambridge.org/bibles/warranty** or on request from Customer Services:

North America	*Rest of the world*
email:	email:
USBibles@cambridge.org	directcs@cambridge.org
Tel: 800-872-7423	

Each real leather Cambridge Bible is unique, because the cover material is a natural product and many of the binding processes are hand crafted. This Bible has been made with skill and care from the best and most appropriate materials: if treated with all reasonable care and respect as befits a well-made and valuable article, it will give years of use. However, if you have cause to believe that it suffers from defects in materials or workmanship – that its current condition is inconsistent with normal wear and tear, and is not the consequence of misuse or damage after it came into your possession - you should contact the vendor from which it was purchased. If they cannot offer resolution, contact Cambridge Customer Services for advice. We reserve the right to inspect the book to determine whether it has a genuine manufacturing flaw before considering appropriate remedy.

Cambridge University Press,
Shaftesbury Road, Cambridge CB2 8BS, UK

CHAPTER 5

OVERCOMING ENTANGLEMENTS OF ERROR & DECEIT

2 Peter 2:20 KJV
For if after they have escaped the pollutions
of the world through the knowledge of the
Lord and Saviour Jesus Christ, they are
again ENTANGLED THEREIN, and overcome,
the latter end is worse with them
than the beginning.

The historical context of Peters epistles is based upon two opposing forces, working through false teaching, in order to seduce the saints into error. I'm convinced that error, deception and falsehood are all sources of spiritual pollution for the believer. One group of falseteachers where joined to a sect called the Gnostics. They claimed to have special knowledge into the things of God but joining their band was the only way to get this alleged knowledge.

The Antinomians was the second group. Their doctrine basically gave credence to illicit living. They claimed because of grace, one was free to do whatever whenever. Of course, both perspectives are in error and those who partook of their doctrine would become polluted. These doctrines are still seeking access to the Church today with the intent of defiling the righteous.

I'm agreeing with you for our Father to expose the operation of doctrinal error and seductive teaching. May His fire root out and dismantle these strong holds in Jesus Name. May your life be free from their works and your soul liberated from any potential entanglements.

LORD, release tenacity upon me to abide indifferent towards the spiritual pollutants of this world.

LORD, purge me of all toxins working within to drive me to former entanglements in Jesus Name.

LORD supply me with the knowledge needed to abide and connect to you. Free me from any enticements to bind me in Jesus Name.

I decree a renewed wit, manifesting and empowering me, to rise above the tactics of hell activated to contaminate me.

I renounce all backsliding demons manifesting to breach my spirit in Jesus Name.

LORD, arise and scatter every twisted thing working to seduce me into entanglements.

I receive knowledge for deliverance as it is written the just, through knowledge, shall be delivered.

I renounce all appetites and activities working to entangle me in Jesus Name.

I renounce any hidden bitterness at work that's serving as a source of entanglement in Jesus Name.

LORD, deliver me from any soul wounds working to entangle me and secure my demise in Jesus Name.

More Great Resources
From Apostle Stephen Garner

- 50 Lessons Ministry Has Taught Me
- Apostolic Pioneering
- Benefits of Praying in Tongues
- Essentials of the Prophetic
- Exposing the Spirit of Anger
- Fervent Prayers
- Fundamentals of Deliverance
- Ministering Spirits: "Engaging the Angelic Realm"
- Pray Without Ceasing, Special Edition
- Restoring Prophetic Watchmen
- Deliver Us From Evil
- Prayers That Strengthen Marriages & Families
- Prayers, Decrees & Confessions for Goodness & Mercy

- Prayers, Decrees & Confessions for Wisdom
- Prayers, Decrees & Confessions for Favour& Grace
- Prayers, Decrees & Confessions for Righteousness
- Prayers, Decrees & Confessions for Prosperity
- Prayers, Decrees & Confessions for Increase
- Prayers, Decrees & Confessions for Rewards
- Prayers, Decrees & Confessions for Peace
- Prayers, Decrees & Confessions for Power
- Prayers, Decrees & Confessions for Healing
- Strife the Enemy of Advancement
- The Blessing
- The Kingdom of God

Contact Information

Visit Our Online Ministry Bookstore @
www.sagministries.com
Email: sagarnerministries@gmail.com
Email: sagarnermedia@gmail.com

Made in the USA
Las Vegas, NV
16 October 2022